START

A NEW BEGINNING TODAY...

Birister Sharma

Copyright © 2022 Birister Sharma

All Rights Reserved.

Dedicated to my loving wife....

Pallabi Devi Sharma

I surrendered to you, O my Lord......

"Om Namah Shivaya"

Table of Contents

One Word

Many times you have heard that time and tide wait for none. It is very rightly said.

Time and tide always follow their own flow and pace. They have no time to wait for anybody or anything. In a similar way, our life is. Our life is a continuous process that began its journey right from our birth and ends with our death; it needs continuous flow and pace. If we ever try to halt its flow and pace, then it wouldn't halt for us, because it is the rule of our life. It always maintains its own flow and pace. If there is life, there is flow and pace. If there is no life, there is no flow and no pace. Life means continuous flow and pace. The moment the flow and pace of life halt, then at that very moment, there is a sudden death end.

Therefore, always follow the flow and pace of your life. Don't miss it. Control your life. Manage your life. Maintain your life. Balance your life. And keep the momentum of your life. This is the rule of your life.

Whatever you want to do in your life, do it today.

Whatever you want to think in your life, think it today.

Whatever you want to plan in your life, plan it today.

Whatever you want to dream in your life, dream it today.

Whatever you want to act on in your life, act on it today.

Whatever you want to work on in your life, work on it today.

2

___***___

1. Think Today!

Think today! Act today! Live today!

Man is a thinking animal. Only man can think. Only you can think.

You're the by-product of your own thinking.

As you think, so you become in your life.

You've got to think to make your life go from good to better, and from better to best.

Nobody can think for you. You've got to think for yourself.

Without thinking, you can't make yourself a better person in your life. Without thinking, you can't live your life.

Thinking gives you new thoughts, new ideas, new creativity, new plans, new strategies, new decisions, and new directions in your life.

Thinking helps you grow and develop yourself both internally and externally.

When you think, you'll know yourself better and better.

You'll evolve into a new and better person in your life.

Thinking helps you to mold yourself completely.

It is only thinking that helps you to solve your problems.

If you think deeply, you'll not only judge yourself but also judge everybody and everything.

If you think, your inner vision and inner self will wake up.

There is great energy and power in your thinking.

If you think, you'll know what is going on inside you and outside you. You'll become more conscious of yourself.

Your thinking will sharpen your wisdom, knowledge, and intelligence.

You have to think every moment and every time.

You have to think about yourself in order to improve yourself.

You have to think about your loved ones.

You have to think about your family.

You have to think about your friends.

You have to think about your relatives.

You have to think about your neighbors.

You have to think about everybody.

You have to think about this world.

Your thinking is a never-ending process.

Think again and again. Re-think again and again.

Think before you do anything. If possible, think one hundred times before you undertake anything at hand.

Think before you see anything.

Think before you hear anything.

Think before you eat anything.

Think before you drink anything.

Think before you speak anything.

Think before you do anything.

Think before you go anywhere.

Think before you stay with anybody.

Your thinking helps you to prepare yourself before anything happens in your life.

Your thinking scrutinizes you before you proceed with anything.

It will scan you thoroughly like an antivirus.

It will sterilize your mind, heart, and soul.

It is like your teacher; it will teach you before the exams of your life.

It is like your guide; it will guide you before unfolding the real world.

A thinking man never commits any mistakes in his life.

Always think practically and logically, but never think emotionally. Because when you think emotionally, you'll think with your heart, and there is a hundred percent chance of making the wrong decision with your emotional heart. On the other hand, if you think practically, you'll think with your brain, and there is a hundred percent chance of making the right decision with your intelligent mind.

Believe in your thinking.

Judge your thinking.

Check your thinking.

Re-check your thinking.

Analyze your thinking.

Then go with your thinking.

A wise man always thinks before he acts on anything; therefore, he hardly commits any mistakes in his life. On the other hand, a foolish man never thinks before he acts on anything; therefore, he always commits many mistakes and falls into the ditch of big troubles in his life.

It is only thinking that makes you wise and intelligent.

Without thinking, you'll become a fool and stupid.

Always think well of yourself.

Never think poorly of yourself.

Because the way you think about yourself is the way you find yourself.

Always think well of your loved ones.

Never think poorly of them.

Because the way you think about them is the way you find them.

Always think well of your family.

Never think poorly of them.

Because the way you think about them is the way you find them.

Always think well of your relatives.

Never think poorly of them.

Because the way you think about them is the way you find them.

Always think well of your friends.

Never think poorly of them.

Because the way you think about them is the way you perceive them.

Always think well of your neighbors.

Never think poorly of them.

Because the way you think about them is the way you perceive them.

Always think well of everything.

Never think poorly of everything.

Because the way you think is the way you perceive everything.

Everything reflects back to you the way you think, because your thinking is like a boomerang. Therefore, always be careful while you think about anything.

If you think good about yourself, you'll become good.

If you think great about yourself, you'll become great.

If you think strong about yourself, you'll become strong.

If you think weak about yourself, you'll become weak.

If you think rich about yourself, you'll become rich.

If you think poor about yourself, you'll become poor.

If you think intelligent about yourself, you'll become intelligent.

If you think wise about yourself, you'll become wise.

If you think a fool about yourself, you'll become a fool.

If you think confident about yourself, you'll become confident.

If you think positive about yourself, you'll become positive.

If you think negative about yourself, you'll become negative.

If you think successful about yourself, you'll become successful.

If you think a failure about yourself, you'll become a failure.

If you think you can do anything, then you can do anything in your life.

There is tremendous energy and power in your thinking.

Your thinking can change you.

Your thinking can transform you from an ordinary person to an extraordinary person.

Therefore, never think of yourself as inferior or mediocre in your life, even in your wildest dreams.

Always keep in mind that you're the by-product of your own thinking; you'll become the way you think.

If you think to win today, then you'll definitely win today.

Whatever you want to do in your life, think today and act today.

You'll always achieve your grand success the right way.

Never leave anything for tomorrow.

Never procrastinate anything that you can do today.

You'll never predict anything that will happen tomorrow.

Think big things, you'll achieve big things.

Think small things, you'll achieve small things.

The way you think is the way you achieve.

The way you think is the way you become.

Be aware of your thinking!

Thinking shapes what you want to do in your life.

Thinking shapes what you want to become in your life.

Your thinking is the outline of your reality.

Think cautiously.

Think analytically.

Everything depends on your thinking.

Think today!

Act today!

___***___

2. Plan Today!

Plan means a clear chart of your life; a way of acting throughout for your bright future.

Your plan is a roadmap of your future endeavors or works, and whatever you want to do in the coming days, weeks, months, and years. Plan today so that you'll make something great in the coming days, weeks, months, and years in your life.

If you want to ride the vehicle of your life merrily and contentedly, then you've got to plan right from today.

Planning plays a very significant role in your life because, without planning, you can't do anything properly. Planning makes you disciplined and keeps you committed in your life. Planning gives you new thoughts and new tactics about your work and your life.

Planning gives you new ideas and new ventures for your successful life.

Planning helps you judge yourself and evaluate your caliber.

Planning gives you proper directions and execution in your life.

Planning is a major part of success in your life.

A man without planning can't do anything or achieve anything in his entire life.

Plan now! Plan today! Don't waste your valuable time, because you never know what will happen tomorrow.

Never wait for tomorrow.

Plan today and execute today.

You've only 'today' in your hands.

Don't waste it.

Proper planning is the source of your happiness, prosperity, and success. A happy man is one who is a great planner in his life. Proper planning is the basic foundation of your life. Without proper planning, you'll never maintain your personal and professional life.

When you make a plan before doing anything, you'll know your strong zones and weak zones; you'll get enough time to polish your strong points, and simultaneously you'll get enough time to improve and amend your shortcomings.

When you make a proper plan, you'll get a proper road map of your success missions. Then you can travel anywhere in your life safe and sound and reach the destination of your success in time.

Nothing is possible without proper planning.

Never expect that your first plan will work for you, but you have to make your second plan; if your second plan fails again, then you have to make your third plan, and if your third plan fails again, then once again you have to make your fourth plan, and so on and so forth. In fact, you have to make your plan until you get a glimpse of your grand success.

If your first plan fails, it doesn't mean that it is the end of your life.

Make your second plan.

Make your third plan.

Make your plan again and again until your plan works for you.

One day, one of your plans will definitely work for you a hundred percent.

But never stop making your plans.

Many people give up their best plans only because of the failure of their first plan. Then they never dare to make their second or third plan. Eventually, they never attain any great success in their entire life.

You have to make your plan every moment and every time in your life, whether it is a small plan or a big plan, but you must make a plan about your life. It will work wonders like a magic wand in your life. Always keep in mind that only a small plan will lead to big success, and a big plan will lead to bigger success.

Without making your plans, you can't move a step further in your life. It is only planning that makes everything easy and effortless. By chance, if you try to move your steps forward without making your plan, then you will always find yourself in the claws of many big troubles and hurdles.

The best way to avoid the problems of life is to make your plan before you commit to anything. It'll always help you prepare yourself and engage in self-assessment.

Planning means you're making your own preparations well ahead of the final moves in your life.

Life is like a big game where you'll have to encounter many unseen and unpredictable challenges and incidents. Hence, plan for your life right from now, without making any delay, and then go ahead. Your life is very short, so plan before anything happens in your life. Making your plan is like your life insurance. It is like saving your money in your bank account for your crucial days. It is like booking your movie ticket or train ticket in advance.

When you make a plan for something, that means you're making an assurance to yourself. You'll know what to do; you'll know when to do it; you'll know how to do it; and you'll know when you will accomplish your job.

Your planning is the imperative part of every walk of your life.

If you want to build your own house, then you'll have to plan five or ten years in advance and start saving your money in your bank account. In every field, planning is the first criterion for accomplishment. Make your plan the topmost priority in your life, then proceed further according to your plan; you'll definitely achieve your desired goal.

Many people fail in their life's endeavors because they never make their plans before doing anything. For them, making a plan means wasting time. In fact, they never try to make any plans in their entire lives.

Making a plan means you're scheduling your life within your time frame.

A student never clears his exams if he never makes his study plan before the exam.

A sportsman never wins any match if he never makes his game plan before the match.

A businessman never grows his business if he never makes any business plan.

A man never attains happiness and success in his life if he never makes his life plans.

To win anything in your life, first of all, you've got to make your winning plans.

Your life is like a long journey. If you want a smooth and comfortable journey in your life, then you have to make a plan well before you start your journey; otherwise, you'll be compelled to face a lot of problems throughout your life's journey. Plan well before you undertake anything at hand. Only good planning makes you a perfect and complete person.

Without proper planning, your life will be confined in the midst of chaos and hustle and bustle, and every time you'll suffocate and exhaust yourself.

Think for a moment: what will happen if there are no traffic signals in your town or city? You'll always trap yourself in the middle of crowded vehicles, waiting for many long hours. The traffic signal is a well-managed plan to control the incoming and outgoing vehicles and to avoid and minimize the occurrence of many road accidents.

In the same fashion, in our lives, we need traffic signals in order to control our overflooded wishes and desires, and at the same time, to avoid and minimize encounters with many blunders and mischief.

Proper planning means a proper way of living your life.

Plan when you'll complete your education.

Plan when you'll do your job.

Plan when you'll start your profession or business.

Plan when you'll build your dream house.

Plan when you'll own your first car.

Plan when you'll settle down in your life.

Plan whatever you want to do in your life well ahead of time.

Every great man is a great planner.

Every great winner is a great planner.

Every great achiever is a great planner.

Every great warrior is a great planner.

Today, ask yourself, "Am I a great planner?"

You'll find your own answer.

A planned life is an ordered and disciplined life.

An unplanned life is a disordered, scattered, and undisciplined life.

What do you want in your life?

You have to decide for yourself.

The choice is always yours.

Don't waste your precious time; plan today and move ahead in your life. Your success is always eagerly waiting for you.

Everything is possible if you plan well before you execute.

Take your time.

Think deeply.

Analyze thoroughly.

Plan well.

Then act well.

You'll definitely achieve whatever you want in your life.

Only proper planning will secure your life.

Nobody can do anything without making proper plans.

Your planning is the winning mantra of your life.

Plan today and make your life secure and successful.

___***___

3. Dream Today!

Your dream is your thoughts about your life.

Your dream is your hopes and aspirations about your life.

Your dream is the picture of the three-dimensional form of your future, which only you can preview with your open eyes.

Your dream shows you the clear and colorful pictures of your thoughts, wishes, and hopes—what you exactly want in your life.

Everything is vividly visualized like a movie of your life if you aspire to fulfill your dreams in your reality.

You have every right to dream about your life, and at the same time, you have to realize your dream in your reality.

You have to dream about yourself.

You have to dream about your loved ones.

You have to dream about your family.

You have to dream about your friends.

You have to dream about everything.

You have to dream in order to love yourself.

You have to dream in order to do something special in your life.

You have to dream in order to achieve something great in your life.

You have to dream in order to make your life beautiful.

You have to dream in order to make your world like heaven.

You have to dream in order to make your life happy.

You have to dream in order to make your life content.

You have to dream in order to make your life successful.

You have to dream in order to make your life prosperous.

You have to dream in order to make your life peaceful.

You have to dream in order to make this world a better place to live.

A man who doesn't love himself will never see dreams in his life.

You're alive because you have dreams in your life.

When you see your dreams, you'll do something worthwhile in your life.

If you have a dream, you have aims and objectives in your life.

If you have a dream, you have purpose in your life.

If you have a dream, you have reason in your life.

Your dreams will give you new meaning in your life.

Your dreams will guide you to fulfill your life's goals.

In fact, your dreams are the replicas of your realities in life.

It's only your dream that motivates you to do something good in your life.

It's only your dream that inspires you to work hard to realize your dream in reality.

It's only your dream that enthuses you to grow and prosper in your life.

It's only your dream that encourages you to live your life fully.

But the moment you cease your dreams, you'll halt the flow of your beautiful life.

Where there is a dream, there are new thoughts, new ideas, new plans, new creativity, new works, and new life.

Where there is no dream, there are no thoughts, no ideas, no plans, no creativity, no works, and no life.

You can't live your life without your dream.

Without a dream, your life is colorless and hazy.

Without a dream, your life is black and white.

It's only your dream that transforms your colorless life into a colorful rainbow.

Always see your dreams with your wide open eyes and with your practical viewpoints. Never follow your dreams with a blindfold.

Dream whatever you want to do in your life, no matter whether it is a small dream or a big dream; no matter whether it is possible or impossible.

Nothing is impossible for you if you dare to dream big dreams in your life.

See your dreams every second.

See your dreams every minute.

See your dreams every hour.

See your dreams every day.

See your dreams every week.

See your dreams every month.

See your dreams every year.

You have nothing to pay to see your dreams.

Never stop dreaming in your life.

You have every right to see your glorious dreams.

Your dream is your moral right.

Nobody can steal your dreams from you.

You couldn't dream that one day you'd have a pair of wings and fly like the birds in mid-air. It is an unrealistic dream that is impossible. But if you dream that one day you'll fly in an airplane, then it is a realistic dream that is quite possible.

Always see your dreams in a practical way, but never see your dreams in a fictitious way. Only then will you turn your dreams into your realities.

Always focus on your realistic dreams so that you can fulfill your dreams in reality.

If you dream big, you'll become big in your life.

If you dream small, you'll become small in your life.

If you dream great, you'll become great in your life.

If you dream well, you'll become good in your life.

If you dream badly, you'll become bad in your life.

If you dream high, you'll become high in your life.

If you dream low, you'll become low in your life.

If you dream of success, you'll become successful in your life.

If you dream of failure, you'll become a failure in your life.

If you dream of happiness, you'll become happy in your life.

If you dream of unhappiness, you'll become unhappy in your life.

Only your dreams will shape you in your life.

Make a resolution to see your dreams and turn them into your realities.

All the great men and women of this world are big dreamers. They all dreamt big dreams in their lives, and they all achieved great names and fame.

There is great magic in your dream because as you see your dream, you become it in your real life.

Do you ever think about why so many people couldn't touch the summit of great success and glory in their lives?

The main reason is that they never dare to dream. In reality, they are afraid to see their dreams. They can't believe in their dreams. Actually, they are daydreamers and part-time dreamers. They are not full-time dreamers.

If you only enjoy seeing your dreams, but you have no guts to turn your dreams into realities, then it is completely meaningless. You're just wasting your valuable time.

What do you want to dream in your life?

A big dream or a small dream?

It is always up to you.

What do you want to become in your life?

A daydreamer, a nightdreamer, or a real dreamer?

If you dream big, you'll achieve big, and you'll become big.

But if you dream small, you'll achieve small, and you'll become small.

Believe in your dreams before you realize your dreams in your reality.

See your dreams.

Think about your dreams.

Speak about your dreams.

Feel your dreams.

Visualize your dreams.

Grow your dreams.

Paint your dreams.

Wake up with your dreams.

Sleep with your dreams.

Walk with your dreams.

Plan for your dreams.

Work for your dreams.

These are the ways to turn your dreams into your realities.

If you see a big dream, you'll achieve your big dream.

If you see a small dream, you'll achieve a small dream.

As you see your dream, you achieve it in your reality.

Your dream is very powerful.

Believe in your dream.

You'll become exactly as you see yourself in your dream.

Always remember that a dead man never sees a dream.

You're a living man.

You've got to see your dream.

As long as you live in this world, every moment you've got to see your dream.

But the moment you stop dreaming, you'll become like a dead man.

Your dream is the blueprint of your success and glory in your life.

Dream today!

Work today!

Realize it today!

Attain it today!

---***---

4. Work Today!

Your work is your biggest worship. Never forget this golden mantra in your life. There is no alternative to your work in your life. Only your work guarantees you grand success. Work today, but never worry about its result. This is the only way to live your life. Never postpone your work for tomorrow. You'll never get today's best work tomorrow.

If there is work, there is life, and there is a world. If there is no work, there is no life, and there is no world. No work, no result, no growth, and no development in your life. This is the truth of life. Nobody can live without work. Only your work makes you a perfect and complete man in your life.

Why do you need work in your life?

You need work because your work is the essence of your life.

You work in order to survive in this world.

Your work gives you meaning and purpose in your life.

Without work, you have no meaning and no purpose in your life.

Without work, you will become useless and worthless.

Without work, your life will become directionless.

Without work, your mind will become a devil's workshop.

Your work makes your mind, body, and soul sound and healthy.

Love your work like you love yourself.

Love your work like you love your loved ones.

You'll never feel tired and fatigued if you love your work.

You'll always enjoy your life and your world.

Never take your work as your baggage or bondage.

Take your work as a precious gift of your life and enjoy it.

A man who loves his work never complains about his life; however, a man who hates his work always complains about his life.

It's only your work that turns your every thought, idea, dream, creativity, plan, and decision into action, and then turns it into your reality.

It's only your work that guides you to your path to success.

It's only your work that converts mere soil into golden coins.

It's only your work that unlocks the door to your great fortune.

You never imagine your life without work.

Your work is your life. Your work is your world.

Never try to run away from your work.

Your work is your duty and responsibility.

Your work is the source of your happiness and prosperity.

Do work with your heart and soul, whether it's a small task or a big one.

Never try to differentiate your work on the basis of its shape and dimensions.

Only identify its value and worth.

Always believe in the quality of your work rather than the quantity of your work.

Many people wait for big projects; that's why they lose many of the best opportunities in their lives.

Never wait for big projects, but try to do your best with whatever work your life offers you.

Every big work starts with small steps and small works. Every small step and every small work turn into bigger works. Therefore, try to do every small work in the best possible way.

The great man is one who does every small work in a great way.

Your work is the foundation of your life and world. Your work always pays you; it never betrays you. The way you work is the way you get its result. But it always demands perseverance, persistence, commitment, determination, sacrifice, and great patience from you. Are you ready for that?

You'll be the happiest person in the entire world if you keep yourself busy with your work. If you keep yourself busy with your work, then you have no time to worry and gossip, and you have no time for any unproductive stuff.

A man who always keeps himself busy with his work will never become old and inactive. He will always remain young and active throughout his life.

Do every task in a simple way with great perfection; you'll always achieve great success in your life. You're not known by your name, but you're only known by your great work. Your great work is the identity of your life. It's only your work that helps you to emerge from your hidden talents and skills. A bar of iron will corrode if it is not used for a long period. In the same way, you too will become like a corroded iron bar if you ever try to neglect your work. Idleness and laziness are the two biggest enemies of your work and life. Never allow these two bitter enemies to enter your life. If these pest-like enemies ever start dwelling in your life, they will not only eat you up completely but also make your life hollow and void.

You're born in this world to work and to live.

You're only alive because of your work.

As long as you live in this world, you've got to live with your work.

You never run away from your work.

This is the law of your life.

Your work gives you a new flow in your life.

You never make your life like stagnant water.

You've got to keep your flow of life in order to live.

A man without work never enjoys his life fully.

Always remember that only a dead man has no work.

Love your work.

Live with your work.

Work now, work today!

Never leave your work for tomorrow.

You'll never regain your lost work tomorrow.

Today is the best time to accomplish your work.

Your work cherishes your life and your world.

If you work today, you'll never sleep with an empty belly in your life.

If you work today, you'll be able to fulfill all the basic needs of your life. Your work is the source of everything. Your work makes your life like heaven. Work today! Live today!

___***___

5. Smile Today!

Your smile is the most beautiful emotion of your pious heart and soul.

Your smile is like a shining jewel on your face. It is like the first rays of the rising sun.

Wear it in every moment of your life.

Look at a small flower at the roadside; it always passes its sweet and gentle smile to everyone, even in harsh weather conditions.

Look at a small kid and how it smiles beautifully.

Be like a small flower and a small kid, and pass your sweet and gentle smile to everyone in every weather condition of your life.

Always keep your sweet smile alive, no matter what happens in your life.

It's the sweetest language of your heart.

Your smile can bring joy and happiness to everyone.

You don't need to pay any price for your smile.

There is no measure of your sweet smile.

There is great magic in your smile.

Your smile will act as a healing touch in your wounded life.

Your one sweet smile can build good relationships and friendships in your life.

Your smile is like a sweet fragrance of love and respect that will attract everyone.

Your smile is a sign of your clean and honest heart.

Your smile is a sign of your positive state of mind.

It's the magic of your sweet smile that brings a lot of joy and happiness into your life.

Always keep your sweet smile on your face; it'll soften your heart and wear out every stress and strain of your mind, body, and soul.

Your smile gives you a fresh look and a positive attitude.

Your one little smile reveals a thousand positive auras about you.

Pass your sweet and gentle smile every second, every minute, every hour, and every day.

Nobody likes to see your serious and gloomy face.

Everybody likes to see your cheerful and smiling face.

Look at your face in the mirror every day with a smiling face, and ask yourself how you feel.

You'll always feel good and confident.

You'll realize that there is some meaning and purpose in your life.

You'll never love anyone without your smile.

You'll never care for anyone without your smile.

You'll never make friends without your smile.

You'll never live your life without your smile.

Your smile is the essence of your life.

Many people are unhappy and discontented with themselves even though they have everything in their lives because they have forgotten their actual smiles.

What about you?

Your smile is the source of your joy and happiness. It is your unique asset; the more you give it, the more you earn from it.

In a small town, two shopkeepers were running their sweet shops adjacent to each other. The first shop was very well-known in the entire town despite the fact that the shopkeeper charged a high price for his sweets, but everybody loved to buy them.

On the other hand, the second sweet shop was not running well, even though the best sweets were available at a cheap price.

One day, somebody asked the people about the reason.

Then the people answered candidly that they actually didn't like the sweets from the first shop, but they liked the shopkeeper because of his sweet, smiling behavior.

On the other hand, despite the best sweets being available in the second sweet shop at a cheap price, the people didn't like the shopkeeper because of his moody and rude behavior. Therefore, it is rightly said that a man without a smile never opens a shop.

A man without a smile never lives a happy and contented life.

Your smile keeps you happy and content.

Your smile keeps you positive and energetic.

Your smile keeps your mind cool and calm.

Your smile keeps you fresh and alive.

Your smile is the identity card of your beautiful life.

Whenever you speak to anyone, always speak with your sweet smile. Whenever you meet anyone, always meet with your sweet smile. Whenever you greet anyone, always greet with your sweet smile. Then see the magical power of your sweet smile. You can captivate everyone with the magical charms of your sweet smile.

In the fairy tales, it is always depicted that an angel wears a sweet smile on her face; however, a devil always wears a bitter smile on his face. What do you like to wear in your real life—an angel face or a devil face? You have to decide for yourself.

Our life is full of troubles and challenges. This is the reality of our lives. We can't escape from these odds of life. But if we keep our smiles on our faces every moment, then everything will become easy for us, and we'll be able to tackle every tough situation in our lives.

Always keep your sweet smile alive, no matter what challenges and circumstances try to overpower and surround you in your life. It is a fact that if you give one small smile to anyone, in return, you'll receive a thousand times more happiness and contentment in your life.

Never forget to smile in your life. Your smile is the beauty of your life. It's only your smile that makes your life beautiful and blissful. Never allow it to fade away. Keep it alive. Keep it for eternity.

You're like a painter of your own life. You can paint whatever you like in your life. If you want to paint a smiling face, then you can paint a smiling face. On the contrary, if you want to paint a gloomy face, then you can paint a gloomy face. Everything depends on you.

Your smile is like a blooming flower,

sweet and fragrant.

It adorns your life and your world.

Your smile is like a sparkling jewel,

cute and beautiful.

It is the beauty of your life.

It is the magic of your world.

It is precious and priceless.

It is a source of your joy and happiness.

Wear it wherever you go and wherever you live.

Never allow it to fade away from your life.

Keep it alive in your life.

Keep it in your heart and soul.

Your smile is the most valuable asset of your life.

Always fill your life and your world with the sweetness of your smile.

Smile today. Live today.

___***___

6. Enjoy Today!

Enjoy your life today!

Who knows whether you will enjoy your life tomorrow or not?

Make today a special and memorable moment, and celebrate with an open heart and soul.

Enjoy your life. Enjoy your world.

Enjoy your work. Enjoy every moment.

Because time and tide wait for nobody.

You have every right to enjoy your life. Nobody has the right to stop you from enjoying your life.

Enjoy yourself.

Enjoy your loved ones.

Enjoy your family members.

Enjoy your friends.

Enjoy your neighbors.

Enjoy your colleagues.

Don't keep yourself too busy in your work that you forget yourself and miss the best opportunity to enjoy your life.

Today is your golden day; enjoy your day with heartfelt content.

Love yourself and enjoy your life fully.

Enjoy your good days.

Enjoy your bad days.

Enjoy your success.

Enjoy your failure.

Maintain yourself in every situation in life.

Keep the balance in your life.

Never forget that your life is always in the midst of happiness and sorrow. This is the reality of your life. You can never deny it.

Many people complain that they have no time to enjoy their lives, but they often forget that they have to manage their time to enjoy their lives. Nobody gets one hundred hours every day; everybody gets only twenty-four hours. In these allotted twenty-four hours, we have to do our work and manage everything in our lives.

They also complain that they have so many problems in their lives; how could they enjoy their lives? But they have always forgotten that problems are a part of their lives. Nobody will escape from the problems of life. They have to solve their problems every day while balancing and enjoying every moment of their lives.

They also start comparing themselves with other successful people around them, and they feel like failures in their lives. But they never try to understand why these people are successful.

They think that money will give them enjoyment and satisfaction in their lives.

So, they are always running after money to accumulate it in their purses or in their bank accounts.

Always keep in mind that money will never give you full enjoyment and satisfaction in your life. Money is only a source of enjoyment, but not actual enjoyment.

Let us suppose that you've booked a movie ticket, but you have no time to watch it. Can you watch a movie? Can you enjoy it without watching? Money can only buy you a movie ticket, but not the enjoyment. You have to manage yourself.

Enjoyment is an art of life. It comes when you are able to manage yourself and your time in a proper manner.

Actually, we've built the four walls of an inferiority complex for ourselves, and we have all enclosed ourselves in it, starting to complain about everything.

'We don't have this thing. We don't have that thing.' And blah and blah... And we start complaining about so many uncountable things one after another.

We've closed the doors of our happiness and enjoyment ourselves and started blaming our fates and the changing situations.

Joy and happiness are like a season at every time.

You can enjoy your life whenever you like; you can enjoy your life wherever you like.

But you have to choose for yourself. The final decision is always yours. You have to take your own initiatives.

It is up to you what you want in your life: an enjoyable life or a sorrowful life.

Think for a moment: without joy and happiness in your life, can you live your life?

Joy and happiness are a part of your life.

They are the basic needs of your emotional well-being.

Without enjoyment, you'll die emotionally and mentally.

Without enjoyment, your life will become haunted and engulfed with never-ending agonies, anger, stress, fatigue, tension, and frustration.

A small child always enjoys equally whether it plays with a small toy or a big toy; it even enjoys playing with a small stick or a dried leaf. It never complains about anything. It just enjoys the moment. It never differentiates between anything. Everything is equal for a small child.

What about you?

If you really want to enjoy your life, then try to enjoy every little thing in your life like a small child. Never differentiate between anything.

We are always looking for the big things in our lives while forgetting many small and wonderful things. That's the main reason for our anxieties and sorrows.

Don't look for big joy and happiness in your life.

Make every small joy and happiness into bigger joy and happiness.

Many people get enough time to criticize others; they have a lot of time to gossip about disgraceful things; they have a lot of time to spread rumors; they have a lot of time to feel jealous of other people's success and progress; they have a lot of time to accuse and curse others, but, unfortunately, they have no time to enjoy their lives fully. They have no time to learn good wisdom and knowledge. They have no time for self-improvement and self-development. And it is unfortunate that they couldn't manage a few seconds of time for the upliftment of their lives.

Your life is how short or how prolonged.

Nobody can predict it.

You've only twenty-four hours in your hands.

You've to use a few seconds for yourself.

You've to manage a few minutes for yourself.

You've to spend a few hours for yourself.

Today's time is yours.

The sand of time never waits for you.

Once it slips away from you,

You'll never regain it tomorrow.

Today is your golden day.

Enjoy your life.

Enjoy your world.

You have every right to enjoy your life fully!

___***___

7. Forgive and Forget Today!

Always follow the mantra of "forgive and forget" in your life today. It'll play like magic in your life. You'll always be happy and content. Forgiveness is the strength of a brave heart. Life is for two days; forgive everybody and forget everything, regardless of the deeds they have done to you and the ways or manners in which they have treated you. Just forgive and forget them and move ahead in your life.

However, it is not an easy job to do. But for the sake of your own benefit, you've got to forgive everybody and forget everything. Otherwise, it'll only harm you. You'll burn yourself in the blazing fires of hatred, anger, and vengeful intentions. You'll become your own victim. Therefore, it is better to forgive everybody and forget everything.

Forgiveness is a pious emotion in which there is no bitter hatred or regret for anybody.

Forgiveness is your strength.

Forgiveness is your act of humility.

It is your noble deed.

It is an act of a brave person.

It is an emotion of love and respect.

There is no difference.

If you forgive someone, it means you understand that person.

You're mature enough in your life.

Forgive and forget everyone for your own happiness.

Forgive and forget everyone for your own love.

Forgive and forget everyone for your own life.

Forgive and forget everyone for your own mental stability and peace.

If you forgive and forget somebody for their misdeeds, then you're helping yourself. If you can't forgive and forget them, then you'll burn yourself in the lava of hatred, anger, and vengeance. You'll become revengeful. It'll only steal your happiness and mental peace. Your life will come to a sudden halt and disrupt everything. It'll become like self-mutilation. If you forgive and forget others' mistakes, differences, and misunderstandings, then only will they do the same for you. But first of all, you've to take your own initiative. It is like you can't clap with one single palm of your hand; you've to join both palms of your hands in order to clap. Ask yourself what you want in your life.

In your life, sometimes or on any occasion, you may encounter anger, hatred, jealousy, betrayal, accusations, curses, and criticism from your beloved ones, family members, friends, neighbors, office colleagues, and strangers. Never react to any of them.

Never take anything seriously. Take it lightly. Handle it with coolness and calm. Try to avoid and ignore them. Forgive and forget everybody and everything as if nothing has happened. Take it as your nightmare. Start a fresh move in your life. Keep yourself busy with your chosen work.

This is the best way to counter them.

On the contrary, if you try to react to everybody and everything, you will never find happiness and contentment in your life; you will just trap yourself in the webs of agony, trouble, and disturbance. And you will turn your beautiful life into a chaos of hell.

You'll burn yourself in the fire of their anger.

Then, you'll lose your own happiness and mental peace.

Avoid and ignore their anger.

Never allow it to dwell in your life.

You'll hurt yourself in the thorns of their hatred.

Then, you'll lose your own love.

Avoid and ignore their hatred.

Never allow it to dwell in your life.

You'll fall down into the ditch of their jealousy.

Then, you'll lose your own honesty.

Avoid and ignore their jealousy.

Never allow it to dwell in your life.

You'll victimize yourself in the mud of their accusations.

Then, you'll lose your own humility.

Avoid and ignore their accusations.

Never allow it to dwell in your life.

You'll deceive yourself in the curse of their betrayals.

Then, you'll lose your own faithfulness.

Avoid and ignore their betrayals.

Never allow it to dwell in your life.

You'll trap yourself in the jaws of their criticisms.

Then, you'll lose your own common sense and instinct.

Avoid and ignore their criticisms.

Never allow it to dwell in your life.

If you react with everybody and everything, then there will be no difference between you and them. You'll lose the vision and mission of your own life. Then you will also try to set your vision and mission only to harm your contemporaries. This will be the beginning of war in your life, and it will divert you far away from the vision and mission of your love, happiness, prosperity, and peace. You'll become like the enemy commander-in-chief and soldier for your own dear ones and peers. You're on the path of your own self-destruction. Your life will become like a battle, and your beautiful world will become like a deadly battlefield.

Many relationships and many families are broken up only because they couldn't forgive and forget one another for their past mistakes, differences, and misunderstandings. They create their own boundaries and become bitter enemies of one another. As a matter of fact, they never want to bow down before one another. They raise questions like: "Why should I? Why me? Why should we?" The problem lies in their egos. They never want to give up their egos. They never want to bow their heads in humility. They want to exhibit their own power and superiority. They are scared of losing their pride and prestige. But, in reality, they have forgotten that directly or indirectly, they are committing a great blunder in their own lives.

If you ever exhibit your humbleness and humility, you'll never lose your pride and prestige; in fact, you're helping yourself while handling the bitter situation. A happy and peaceful life is only possible if you forgive and forget the past mistakes, differences, and misunderstandings of your dear ones and peers, and when you focus on your vision and mission in new perspectives.

Forgive and forget each other's mistakes, differences, and misunderstandings, amend them today, and move ahead in your life.

Forgive and forget is the best solution to solve every past mistake, difference, and misunderstanding in your life. Forgive and forget is the only way to mend every broken relationship.

If you have bitter differences with your dear ones,

Then forgive and forget each other right now.

You'll get nothing in hatred and anger.

You'll get nothing in jealousy and revenge.

You'll get nothing in accusations and criticisms.

Rebuild your broken relationships.

Unite with each other.

Love and care for each other.

Respect and understand each other.

Praise and inspire each other.

Start a new beginning.

And live together with happiness, peace, and harmony.

---***---

8. Love Today!

Love is the most beautiful emotion in this entire world.

Every living creature understands and feels love.

Love is the universal language that expresses everything; even birds and beasts can comprehend it easily.

Love is the only bond that ties everybody together.

It's the foundation of love that unites us in our families and in our society.

Love is eternal.

If you love somebody, in return, you'll receive love.

Love is the mother of everything.

If there is love, there is joy and happiness.

If there is love, there is respect and understanding.

If there is love, there is oneness and unity.

If there is love, there is peace and prosperity.

If there is love, there is compassion and mercy.

If there is love, there is only joy and happiness; there is no place for unhappiness, hatred, anger, egos, jealousies, vengeance, division, and disturbance.

Love yourself before you love somebody. When you know how to love yourself, only then will you know how to love other people.

There is great power in love.

Only love can change you; only love can change your life and your world.

With your love, you can win every battle of your life.

Only love can build the foundation of your relationship.

Only love can construct the bridge of your friendship.

Only love can mend every broken heart and relationship.

Only love can heal every wounded heart.

Without love, you can't live in this world.

And nobody can live without love.

Love is the antidote to every emotional ailment.

You're surviving in this world only because of love.

Without love, your life is meaningless.

Without love, your life is colorless.

It's only love that gives you new meaning and purpose in your life.

It's only love that shows you new ways and new directions in your life.

Life is always a big mystery; nobody knows when it'll come to an end. You have no idea when you will breathe your last.

Life is very short and unpredictable. Therefore, love yourself as much as you can; love your loved ones and family members as much as you can. Today. Now. Nobody knows when the sands of time will halt all of a sudden. Anything can happen at any moment in your life.

In a big city, there once lived a wealthy merchant with his family. He was very rich and prosperous, but he had no time for his loved ones and family members. All the time, he was traveling for his business tours. In a month, he only visited his house once or twice, and then the very next day he would set out for his next business tour.

Many times, his beloved wife and his children asked him to stay with them and spend some quality time, but every time he told them that he was only doing business for their happiness and prosperity, so he had no time at the moment. He promised that when he accumulated more money and wealth for them, he would settle down and spend good time with them forever.

In the same manner, many years passed, but the merchant was still engaged in his business tours. Then, one day he wished to visit his house to meet his beloved wife and children. So, he took a long holiday from his business tours and went to visit his house. He was very happy and excited. He would see his beloved wife and children after a one-year-long gap.

But the day before the merchant was to arrive at his house, a devastating earthquake occurred in the entire city, and everything was destroyed. When the merchant reached his house, he couldn't find it; instead, he witnessed the collapsed debris of his home and the lying dead bodies of his beloved wife and children. The poor merchant wept and repented, but it was too late for him to meet his beloved wife and children alive.

Nobody knows what will happen next; nobody knows what will happen tomorrow, in the coming days, in the coming weeks, in the coming months, and in the coming years. Nothing is predictable. Nothing is in your hands. Anything can happen in your life.

Therefore, whatever you want to do, do it right away. Do it right now. Do it today. Don't wait for the next day. Don't wait for the next week. Don't wait for the next month. Don't wait for the next year.

Love yourself today.

Love your loved ones today.

Love your family today.

Love your friends today.

Love your neighbors today.

Whatever you want to do in your life, do it today.

Whatever you want to give in your life, give it today.

Whoever you want to meet in your life, meet them today.

Whoever you want to see in your life, see them today.

Wherever you want to go in your life, set out today.

Don't leave for tomorrow.

Don't wait for tomorrow.

What you can do today, you can't do tomorrow.

Always remember, tomorrow never comes.

Love today!

Live today!

Make your life full of joy and happiness.

Make your life meaningful and purposeful.

---***---

9. Set Your Goal Today!

A man without a goal is like a bird without wings.

Have you ever seen a bird without wings?

Every bird has wings to fly in the blue sky and to soar the world.

If you have a goal in life, then you can achieve anything; you can soar your achievements everywhere. You can earn name, fame, and wealth in your life.

Set your goal in life. Nobody will help you set your goal.

Only you can set your own goal.

Always keep your goal in front of your eyes.

If you have a goal to become a doctor, then you will achieve your goal.

If you have a goal to become an engineer, then you will achieve your goal.

If you have a goal to become a scientist, then you will achieve your goal.

If you have a goal to become a successful businessman, then you will achieve your goal.

If you have a goal to become a sportsman, then you will achieve your goal.

If you have a goal to become an artist, then you will achieve your goal.

If you have a goal to become an actor, then you will achieve your goal.

If you have a goal to become a singer, then you will achieve your goal.

If you have a goal to become a dancer, then you will achieve your goal.

If you have a goal to become a leader, then you will achieve your goal.

If you have a goal to become rich and wealthy, then you will achieve your goal.

If you have a goal to become a winner, then you will achieve your goal.

If you have a goal to become successful in your life, then you will achieve your goal.

If you have a goal to become powerful in your life, then you will achieve your goal.

If you have a goal, then you'll achieve something in your life. But if you have no goal, then you'll achieve nothing in your life. Without a goal, you're a zero. Your life is useless, meaningless, and directionless. You'll only wander through your life.

It is well said, "Shoot for the moon. Even if you miss, you'll land among the stars."

Ram and Gopal are two best friends. Ram has a goal in his life. He sets his goal every day. He has a vision and mission to chase his goal. He works hard and accomplishes every goal. After ten years, he became a rich and wealthy man in his town. Then he settled down happily in his life. On the other hand, Gopal has no goal in his life. He didn't set any goals. He has no vision and no mission in his life. He was idle and wandered through his life, doing many numerous tasks one after another. He didn't achieve anything. After ten years, his condition was pitiable, like a beggar.

Who do you wish to become like? Ram or Gopal?

Your goal gives you ways and directions in your life. It'll give you new acceleration and new energy. It'll boost your self-confidence, self-belief, self-esteem, and enthusiasm. Set your goal, and then see the magic in your life. It'll completely change and transform you. You'll be compelled to excel in your life. You'll achieve everything and become successful. Your goal makes you responsible and disciplined. Set one specific goal for yourself, and go for it. Success is always yours.

But never make the mistake of setting too many goals at one time; you'll lose your way and wander through life. You'll achieve nothing.

Be like a flowing river.

A river never stops in any place. It is continuously flowing day and night, without getting tired, and finally, it reaches its final goal: confluence with the mighty ocean.

Set your goal, and just follow it. Work hard day and night without getting tired, and you'll definitely reach your goal in the end. Nobody will stop you.

Your goal clarifies your visions and missions in life.

Your goal gives you new meaning and purpose in your life.

Without a goal, you'll never discover your hidden natural skills and talents.

Without a goal, you'll experience frustration, confusion, and tension in your life.

Without a goal, you'll waste your valuable time and life.

All the great men and women who have created significant histories and achievements in their lives have had great goals. They set their great goals from the very beginning and worked hard with high spirits, dedication, and patience, accepting all the odds of life and facing all the tough challenges that came across their paths to success.

Mahatma Gandhi had a goal to liberate his motherland, India, from British rule. He succeeded in his goal.

Nelson Mandela had a goal to free his countrymen from the evil practice of apartheid in South Africa. He succeeded in his goal.

Thomas Alva Edison had a goal to invent an electric lamp. He succeeded in his goal.

The Wright brothers had a goal to invent the flying machine. They succeeded in their goals.

Mother Teresa had a goal to set up a home for the poor and helpless. She established a home called 'Nirmal Hriday' in Calcutta (Kolkata). She succeeded in her goal.

Pele has a goal to become the best football player in the world. So he became the all-time great legend in the game of football.

Sachin Tendulkar has a goal to become the best cricketer. So he became the God of Cricket.

Amitabh Bachchan has a goal to become an actor. So he became the legendary megastar in Bollywood cinema.

Lata Mangeshkar has a goal to become a singer. So she became the melody queen in the singing industry in India.

Michael Jackson has a goal to become a pop singer. So he became the king of pop in the music world.

What is your goal in life?

Ask yourself and figure it out.

You'll achieve great success and glory if you set your goal right from today and from now.

In the game of football, the two teams are always playing against each other for a full ninety minutes.

Let us suppose that there are no goalposts in the playground; then what will happen? How will the players play their match? They will either pass the ball to one another or just shoot the ball into the mid-air. Then who will watch their match? In fact, there will be no match and no audience to support the two teams. There will be no excitement. There will be only boredom everywhere.

Similarly, your life is like a football match. You must have a goal in your life in order to make your life full of thrills and excitement. You should never live your life without setting a goal. Always be a goal-oriented person. Only a goal-oriented person will achieve something great in life. Even a tiny ant has its goal; it gathers a lot of foodstuffs for the winter season. Even a small honeybee has its goal: it aims to collect honey every day from the nectar of flowers while traveling many miles.

Do you have any goals in your life? If not, then please set your goals starting today, right now.

Only your goal will give you new ways and new directions in your life. You'll always be happy in your life if you set your goal. Only your goal will lead you in your life. Only your goal helps you shine in your life.

You'll never start any journey if you're not aware of your destination. Your destination is the goal of your journey. If you travel without knowing your destination, then you'll always lose your way in the middle of the crossroads and wander hither and thither. In the same way, your life is like a journey. You must know your destination before you start your journey of life. Without knowing your destination, you'll never reach anywhere in your life.

A man without a goal is like a dried leaf.

A dried leaf has no destination and no goal; it's always blown away by the wild wind.

Set your goal right from today.

Set your goal right now.

Your goal leads you in your life.

Your goal gives you new ways in your life.

Your goal gives you new directions in your life.

Without a goal, you can't move ahead in your life.

Without a goal, you can't achieve anything in your life.

If you have a goal, then nobody can stop you.

You'll find your vision and mission in life.

You'll discover your hidden potential.

You'll become unstoppable.

You'll reach wherever you want in your life.

You'll touch the summit of every great success and glory.

Never forget to set your goal.

Set your goal right from today.

Set your goal right now.

---***---

10. Live Your Life Today!

Your life always depends on today, but never depends on tomorrow. It's like that if you want to survive for tomorrow, then you've got to keep yourself healthy and wealthy today. Whatever you do today, everything reflects on tomorrow. If you can control your today, then you can control your tomorrow as well as your future. Your tomorrow and the coming days, weeks, months, and years are all under your control. If you make your today successful, then your tomorrow will automatically become successful and grand. If you concentrate on today and devote yourself to your cherished goal, then you've nothing to worry about tomorrow and your future. You'll achieve your goal. Everything depends on today. Your today is the mother of your tomorrow. If you secure your today, then your today will directly secure your tomorrow and your future. Both.

You'll never get today's best moment tomorrow.

Today's best moment is in your hands; you're free to do anything with your today.

Do your best thing in today's time so that you'll get its fruitful results tomorrow and in your coming days, weeks, months, and years.

Those who always think too much and wait for tomorrow, worrying about their futures and doing nothing, cannot achieve anything in their lives. In fact, they are just wasting their precious lives and valuable time.

Don't think too much. Don't worry about anything. Don't wait for anything.

Think and act right now. Today. And forget about tomorrow.

Think and act today and live your best life in today's moment.

You're the king of today.

Rule it with all your might.

Utilize it for your constructive and innovative works.

Never allow it to go to waste.

You're the master of today.

You can do anything with it.

Make your today work in your favor.

Order it to serve you like an obedient servant.

Today you're strong and powerful, but you never know what will happen in the coming days, weeks, months, and years. Therefore, make yourself so strong and powerful that the coming days, weeks, months, and years will never dare to make you weak or sick.

Life is like the changing seasons. Every time, it changes its course. Nobody can stop it. Sometimes it is like a burning summer season full of worries and tensions. Sometimes it is like a freezing winter season full of anxieties and loneliness. Sometimes it is like a colorful spring season full of joy and happiness, success and glory. Sometimes it is like an arduous autumn season full of challenges and upheavals. But you have to maintain and balance your life in every changing season of life. Live in your best moment today. And make your today special and memorable.

Your past is already dead and buried. Forget about it. Your present is just born today. Concentrate on it. Your tomorrow is the by-product of your today. Don't worry about it. Your future is still lying inside the womb of your today. Don't worry about it. Make your today meaningful and purposeful. And live your best life in today's moment.

Always remember that whatever seeds you sow today, you'll reap in your near future. If you take care of your best moments today, then your today will take care of your tomorrow and your future itself.

A strong and positive man always says, "I've only today. I'll do my work today. I have no tomorrow." However, a weak and negative man always says, "I have tomorrow. I'll do my work tomorrow and in the coming days." In reality, tomorrow will never arrive in our lives. When tomorrow arrives in our lives, it will become today.

Never wait for tomorrow. Whatever you want to do in your life, do it today!

Whatever you want to accomplish in your life, accomplish it today! Don't miss the golden opportunity of today. Grab it as soon as it knocks at your door. And give your heart and soul to your work today.

The needle of time is always ticking on and on. It'll never wait for anyone. You've got to go with its pace. If you fail to follow the pace of time, then time will destroy you one day. Nobody knows when your time will come to an end; therefore, use every moment in the best possible manner. Don't be afraid of anything. Be brave! And believe in yourself. Give your best work with dedication and patience. You're bound to achieve your goals in life. Live in your best moment today. You'll always remain happy and content in your life.

If you want to relish your favorite dish, then taste it today.

If you want to watch your favorite movie, then watch it today.

If you want to play your favorite game, then play it today.

If you want to sing your favorite song, then sing it today.

If you want to dance to your favorite beats, then dance today.

If you want to smile the sweetest smile of your life, then smile today.

If you want to crack the funniest jokes of your life, then crack them today.

If you want to laugh to your heart's content, then laugh aloud today.

If you want to enjoy the best moment of your life, then enjoy it today.

If you want to think the best thoughts and ideas in your life, then think them today.

If you want to cultivate the best habits in your life, then cultivate them today.

If you want to see the biggest dreams of your life, then dream them today.

If you want to talk about the best things in your life, then talk about them today.

If you want to visit the best place in the world, then visit it today.

If you want to plan the best plan of your life, then plan it today.

If you want to make the best decision of your life, then decide it today.

If you want to take the best action in your life, then take it today.

If you want to deliver your best work in your life, then deliver it today.

If you want to give your true love to someone, then give it today.

If you want to forgive someone, then forgive them today.

If you want to forget something, then forget it today.

If you want to help someone, then help them today.

If you want to realize yourself, then realize yourself today.

If you want to improve yourself, then improve yourself today.

If you want to create the best thing in your life, then create it today.

If you want to learn something great in your life, then learn it today.

If you want to read the most important thing in your life, then read it today.

If you want to teach a great lesson to someone, then teach them today.

If you want to discover special things in your life, then discover them today.

If you want to celebrate your life, then celebrate it today.

If you want to live your great life, then today is the best time to live it fully.

Always live your life in today's best moment.

Never wait for tomorrow.

Your tomorrow never comes.

Do whatever you want to do today.

Never adjourn anything for the next day. Make your today glorious and successful.

Think today. Work today. Live today.

___***___

About the author

Birister Sharma is a full time author. He is also an avid reader. He loves reading, writing, and motivation. He has penned down dozens of self-help motivational books and novels so far.

You may contact him @ birister2007@gmail.com